The Classical Piano Method

Repertoire Collection 1

Hans-Günter Heumann

ED 13355

www.schott-music.com

Mainz · London · Madrid · Paris · New York · Tokyo · Beijing

ED 13355
British Library Cataloguing-in-Publication-Data.
A catalogue record for this book is available from
the British Library.
ISMN 979-0-2201-3215-5
ISBN 978-1-84761-237-3

Cover design by www.adamhaystudio.com
Cover photography: iStockphoto
Printed in Germany S&Co.8699

CONTENTS

4

1. Merry and Sad

♩ = 100

Hans-Günter Heumann

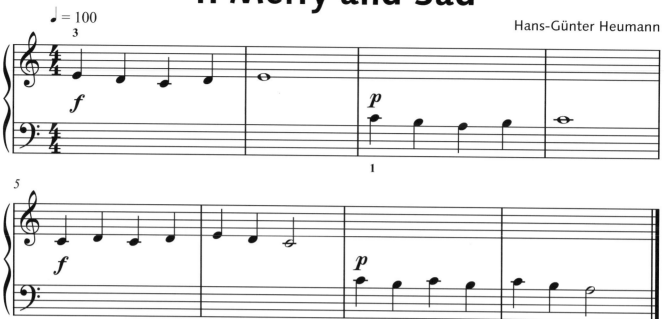

2. Wild Horseman

♩ = 160

Karl Gottlieb Hering (1766-1853)

3. Passion

Hans-Günter Heumann

4. Melody No. 12

from *L'ABC du Piano*

Theme

Félix Le Couppey (1811-1887)

1st Variation

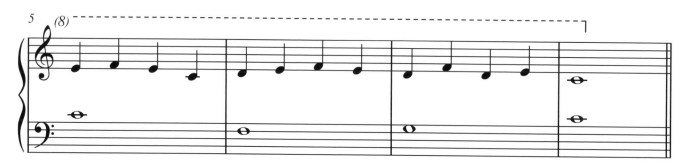

2nd Variation

3rd Variation

5. March

Joseph Küffner (1776-1856)
Arr.: Hans-Günter Heumann

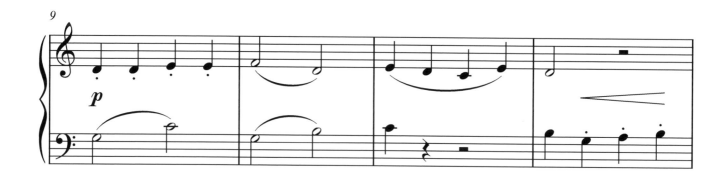

6. Hansel and Gretel

German Folk Song
Arr.: Hans-Günter Heumann

7. Lullaby

Melody from Salzburg
Arr.: Hans-Günter Heumann

8. Rock Fever

Hans-Günter Heumann

9. Oragnia figata fa*

Wolfgang Amadeus Mozart (1756-1791)
Arr.: Hans-Günter Heumann

*) Wolfgang Amadeus Mozart was three years old when he composed this song. Every evening, before going to bed, he jumped onto his father's lap and pulled his ears until he began to hum the second part to this melody. At the end, he received a tender kiss on the end of his nose! The title doesn't make sense, as little Wolfgang made up the language himself. In any case, it sounds amusing and a little Italian.

10. Minuet

from *Notebook for Nannerl*

Leopold Mozart (1719-1787)
Arr.: Hans-Günter Heumann

Moderato ♩ = 116

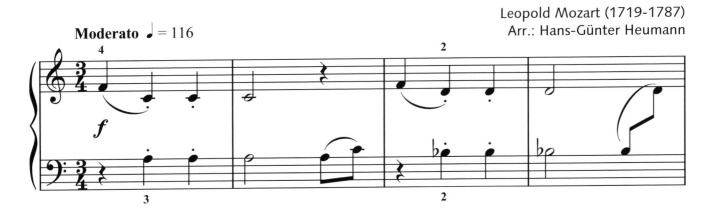

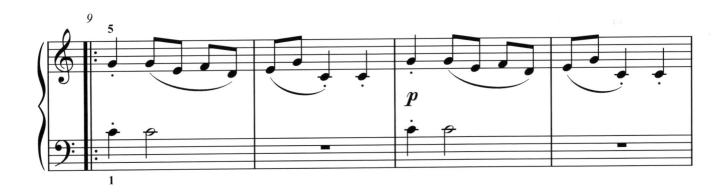

11. For He's a Jolly Good Fellow

French Folk Tune, 1709
Arr.: Hans-Günter Heumann

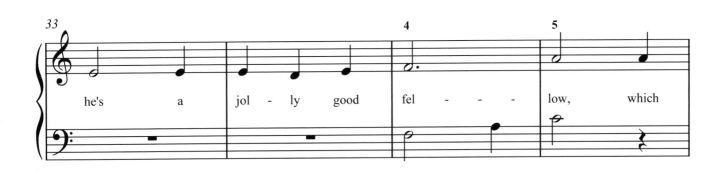

12. Perfect Day

Hans-Günter Heumann

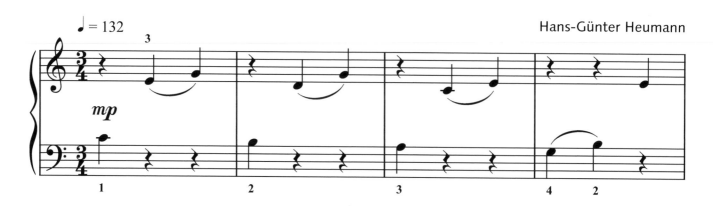

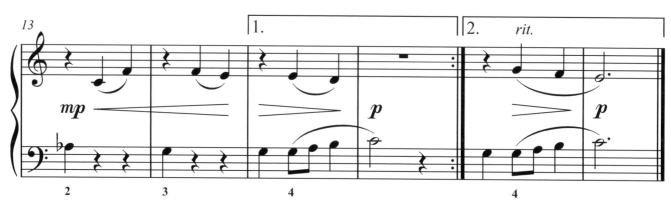

13. Banks of the Ohio

American Folk Song
Arr.: Hans-Günter Heumann

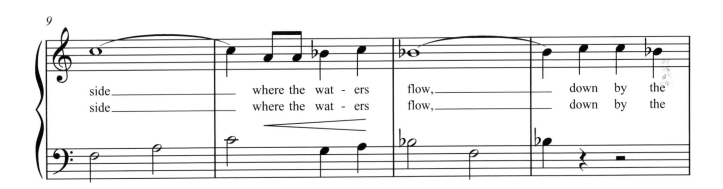

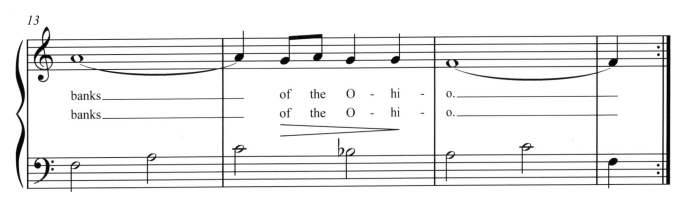

14. The Little Pianist

Op. 823, No. 6 *

Carl Czerny (1791-1857)

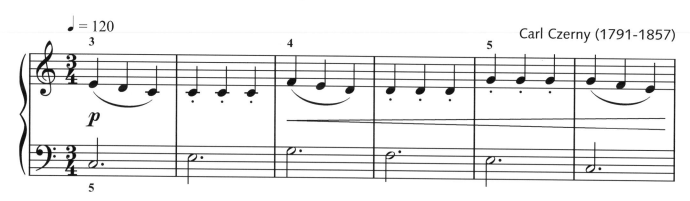

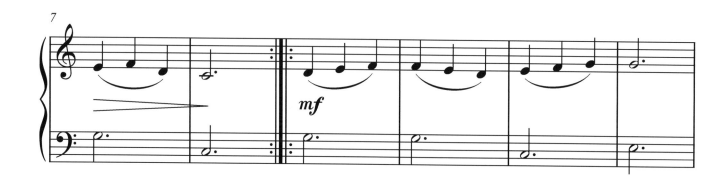

*) Both hands are played one octave higher in its original version.

15. Morning Greeting

from *The First Performance* Op. 210, No. 1 *

Cornelius Gurlitt (1820-1901)

Moderato ♩ = 120

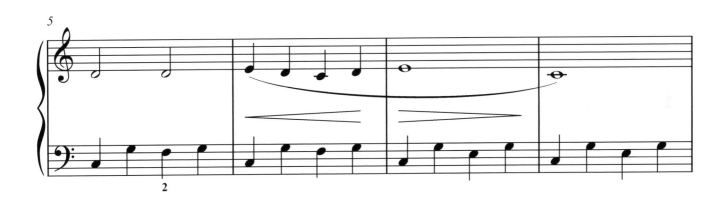

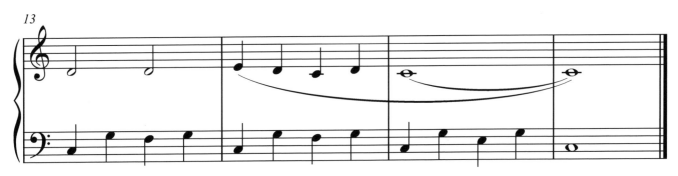

*) Both hands are played one octave higher in its original version.

16. Little Melodic Exercises
for Beginners

Op. 187, No. 13 *

Cornelius Gurlitt (1820-1901)

Op. 187, No. 14 *

*) Both hands are played one octave higher in its original version.

Op. 187, No. 15 *

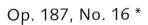

Op. 187, No. 16 *

*) Both hands are played one octave higher in its original version.

17. Lullaby

from *Fireside Fancies* Op. 197, No. 1 *

Moderato ♩ = 120

Cornelius Gurlitt (1820-1901)

*) Both hands are played one octave higher than written in its original version.

18. Buzz, Buzz, Buzz!

From Czech Republic
Arr.: Hans-Günter Heumann

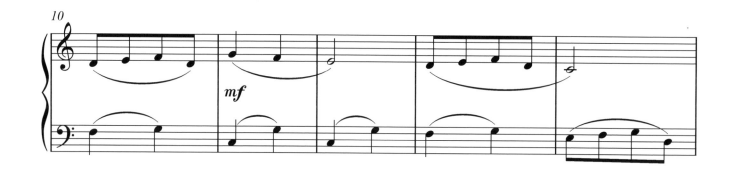

19. When the Saints Go Marchin' In

Traditional
Arr.: Hans-Günter Heumann

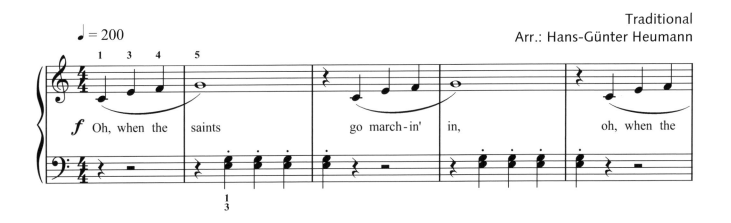

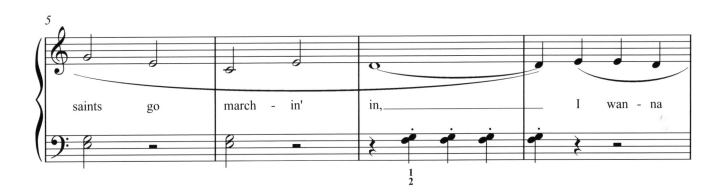

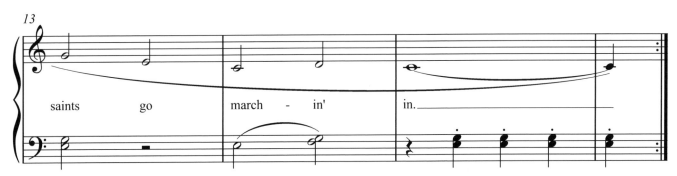

20. Dance at the Royal Court

Hans-Günter Heumann

21. Beethoven Goes Rock

♩ = 80

Hans-Günter Heumann

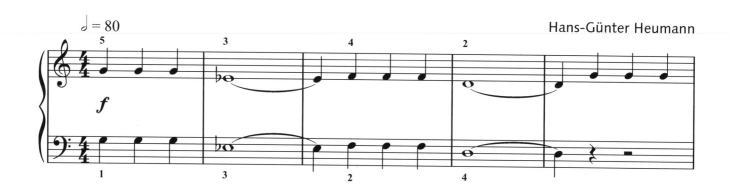

22. Rule Britannia

Thomas Arne (1710-1778)
Arr.: Hans-Günter Heumann

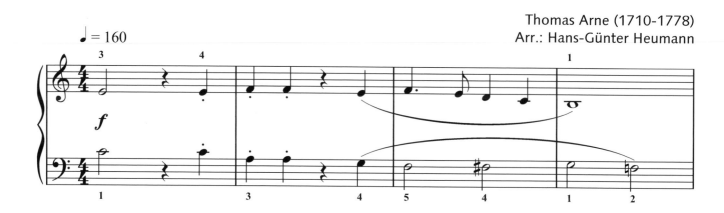

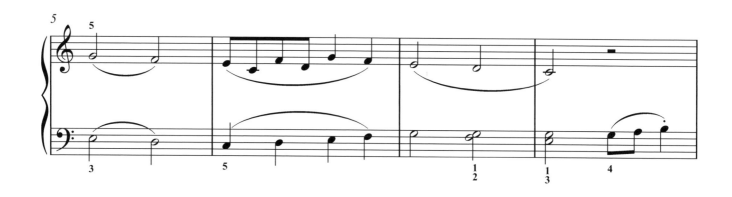

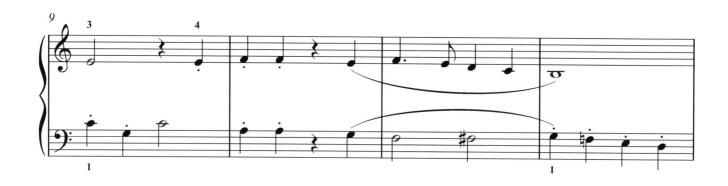

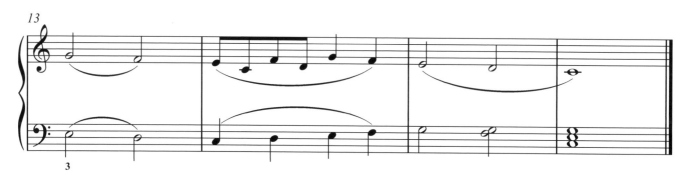

23. Trumpet Voluntary

Jeremiah Clarke (c. 1674-1707)
Arr.: Hans-Günter Heumann

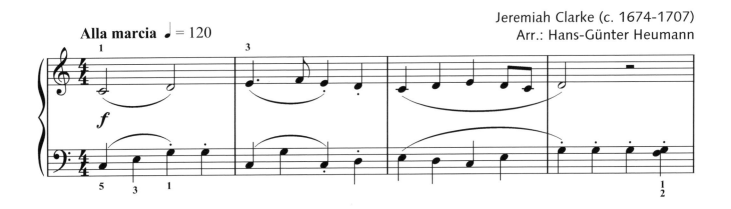

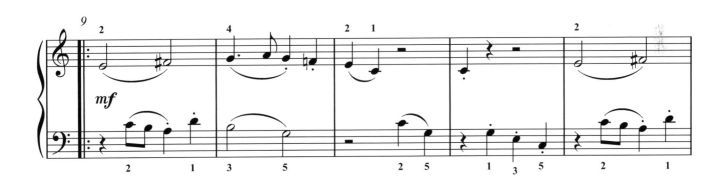

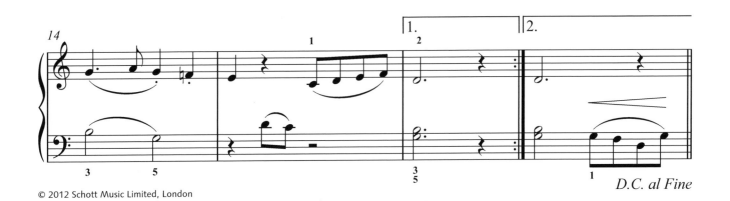

24. Radetzky March

Theme from Op. 228

Johann Strauss, Sr. (1804-1849)

25. Melody No. 15

from *L'ABC du Piano*

Félix Le Couppey (1811-1887)

26. Presto

Daniel Gottlob Türk (1750-1813)

27. Allegro

Daniel Gottlob Türk (1750-1813)

28. That Sound is so Lovely

from the Opera *The Magic Flute*

Wolfgang Amadeus Mozart (1756-1791)
Arr.: Hans-Günter Heumann

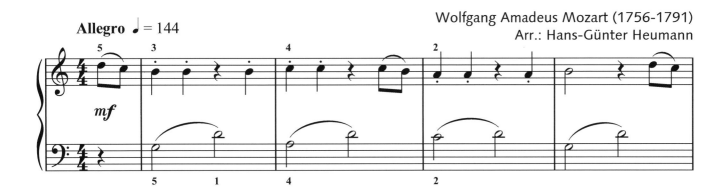

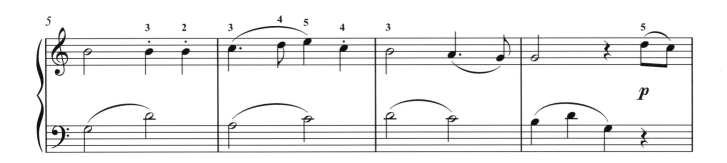

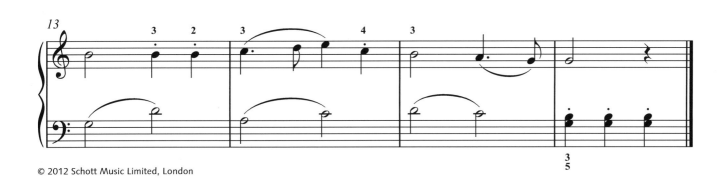

29. Antique Dance

Joachim van den Hove (c. 1570-1620)
Arr.: Hans-Günter Heumann

30. Piano Piece

Op. 101, No. 39

Ferdinand Beyer (1803-1863)

31. Andante grazioso

Theme from the 1st Movement of Piano Sonata K 331

Wolfgang Amadeus Mozart (1756-1791)
Arr.: Hans-Günter Heumann

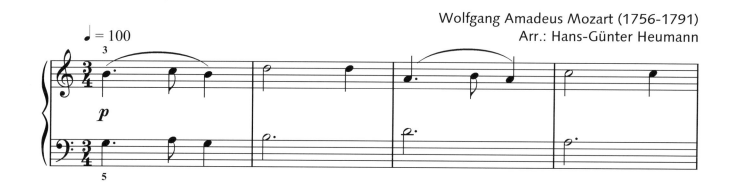

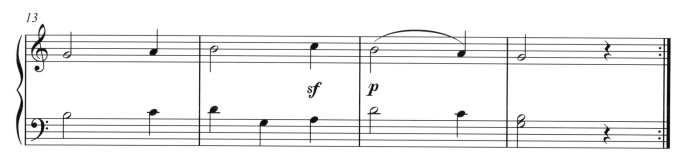

32. The Little Pianist

Op. 823, No. 15

Carl Czerny (1791-1857)
Arr.: Hans-Günter Heumann

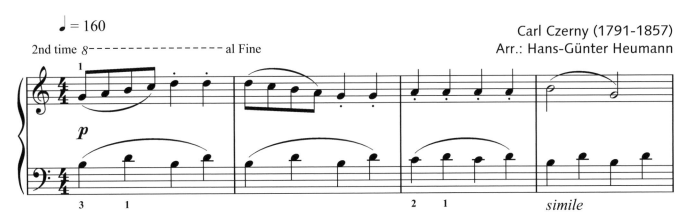

33. Melody

Friedrich Baumfelder (1836-1916)

34. Piano Piece

Op. 101, No. 61

Ferdinand Beyer (1803-1863)

35. Fairytale Melody

Theme with Variations

Theme

German Folk Tune, 18ᵗʰ Century
Arr.: Hans-Günter Heumann

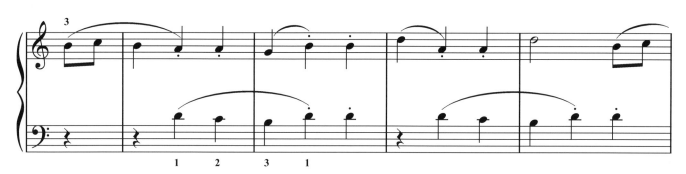

Variation 1

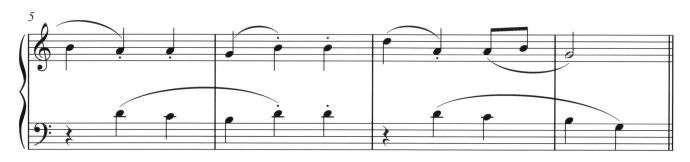

Variation 2

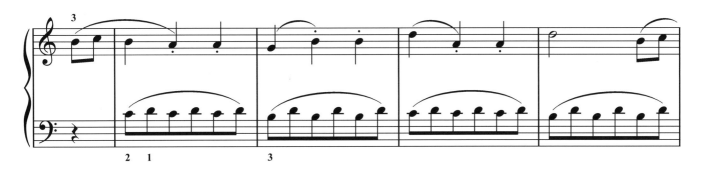

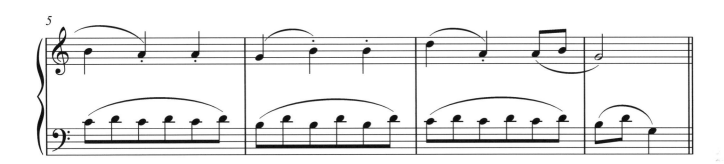

Variation 3

36. The Brave Boy

Op. 197, No. 3

Cornelius Gurlitt (1820-1901)

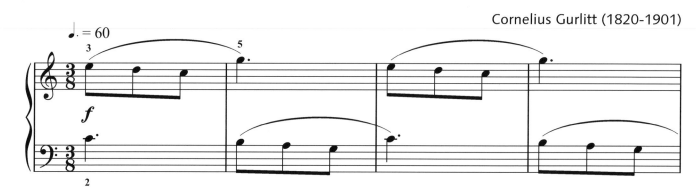

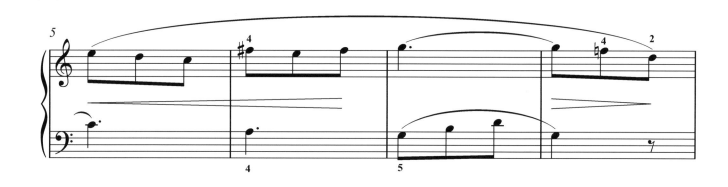

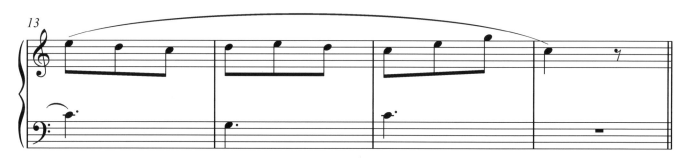

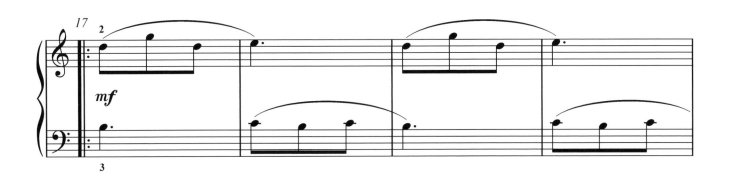

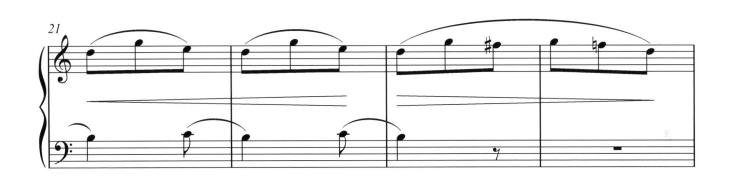

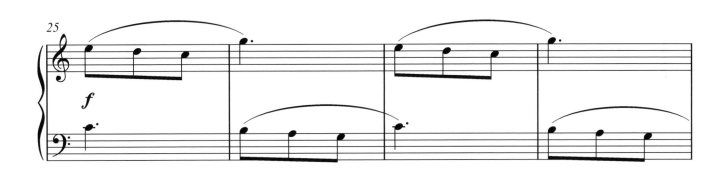

37. Minuet

James Hook (1746-1827)

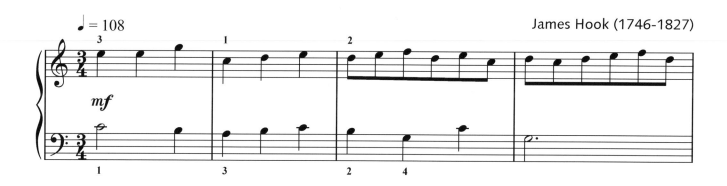

38. Gavotte

James Hook (1746-1827)

39. Waltz

from *Swan Lake*

Pyotr Ilyich Tchaikovsky (1840-1893)
Arr.: Hans-Günter Heumann

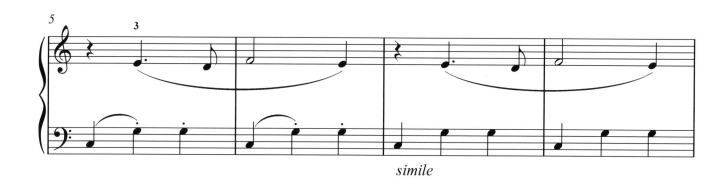

simile

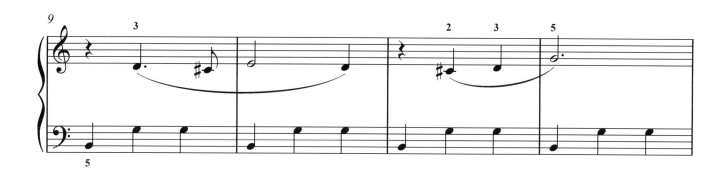

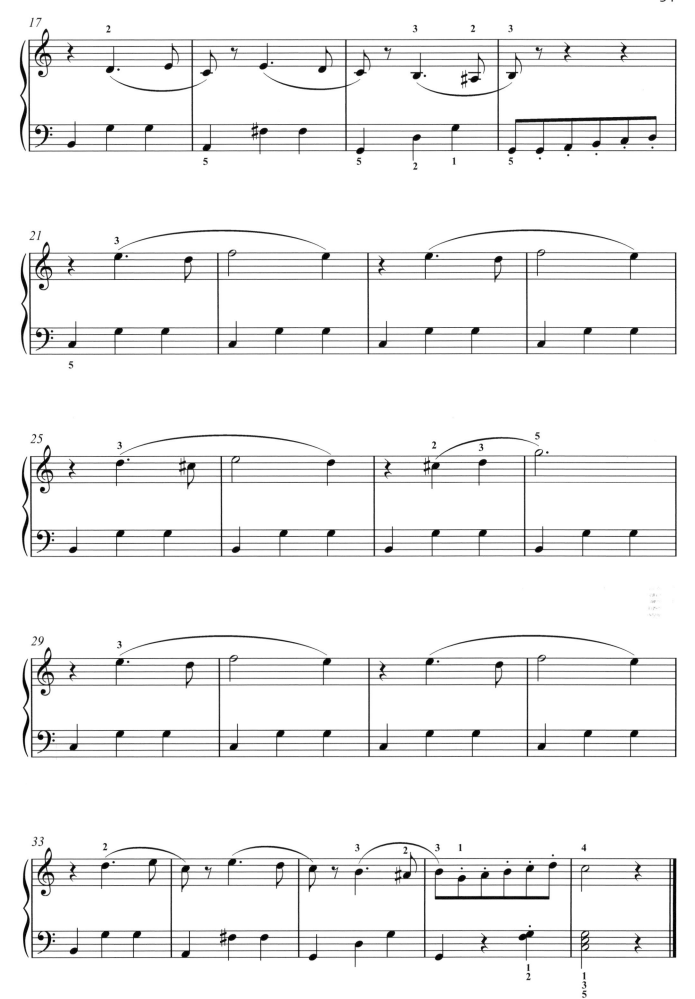

40. Capriccio Italien

Theme from Op. 45

Pyotr Ilyich Tchaikovsky (1840-1893)
Arr.: Hans-Günter Heumann

41. Piano Piece

Op. 101, No. 60

Ferdinand Beyer (1803-1863)

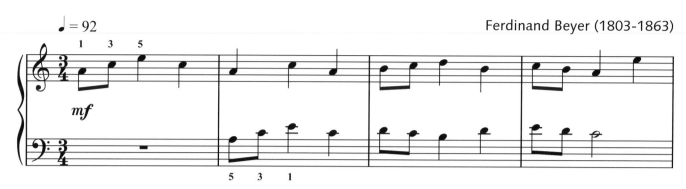

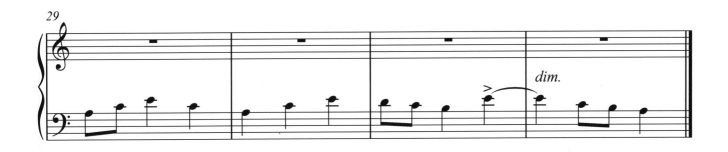

42. Lost in Thought

Hans-Günter Heumann

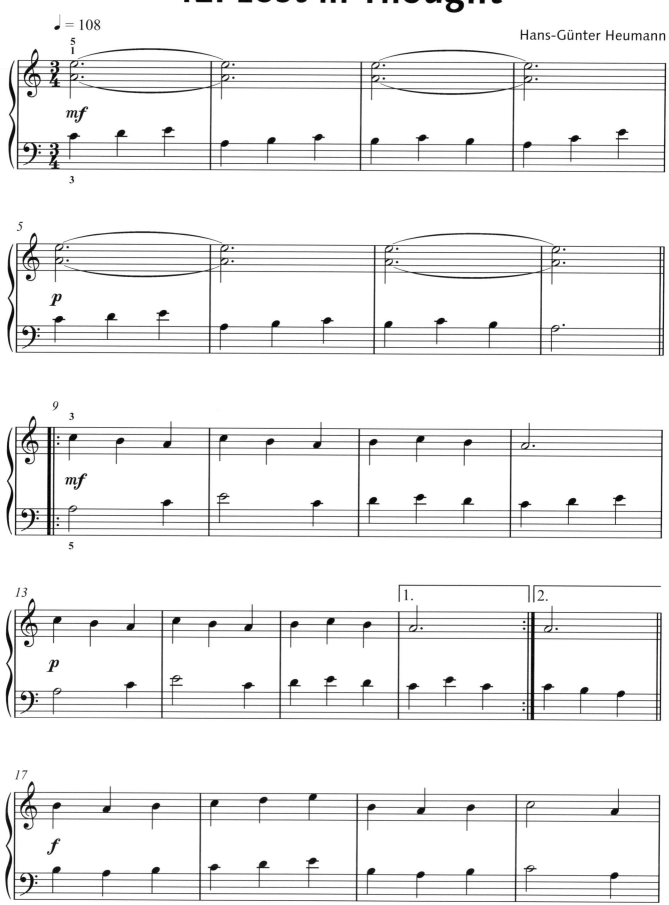

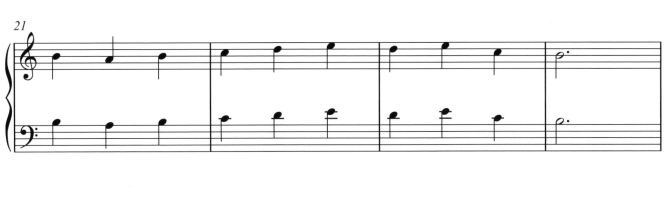

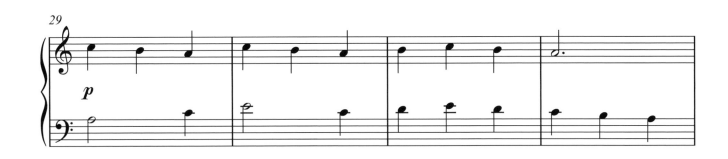

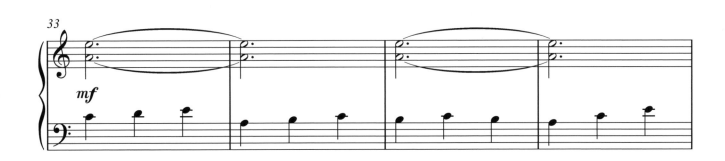

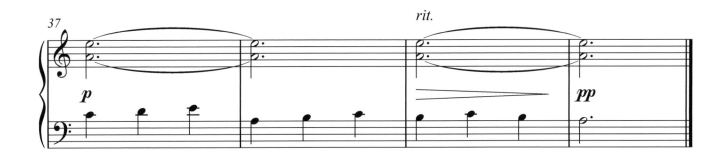

43. Harlequin

Hans-Günter Heumann

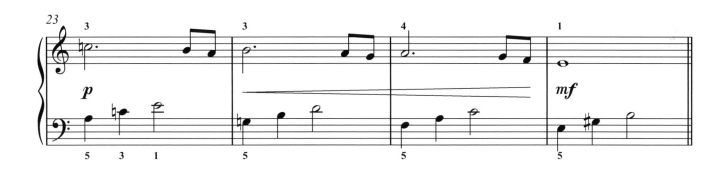

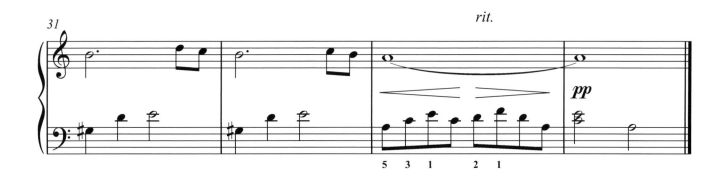

44. Rocky Keys

♩ = 160

Hans-Günter Heumann

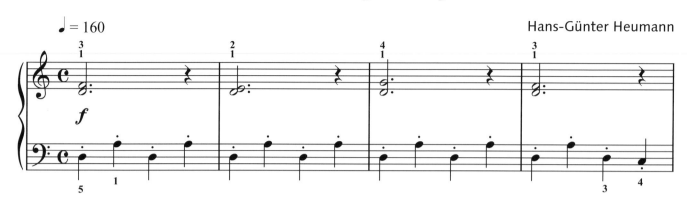

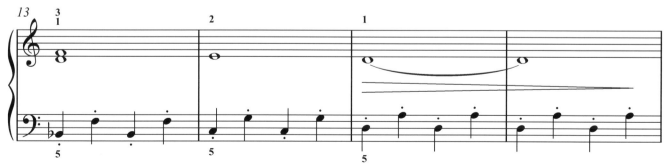

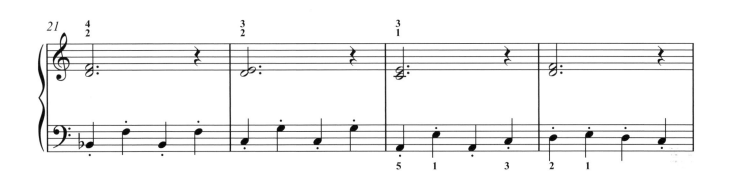

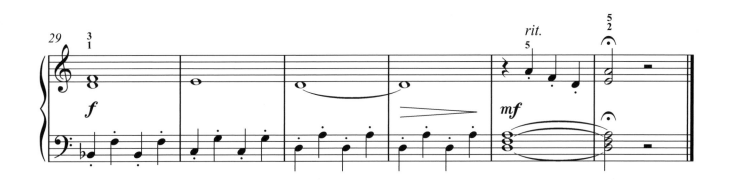

45. Piano My Love

Hans-Günter Heumann

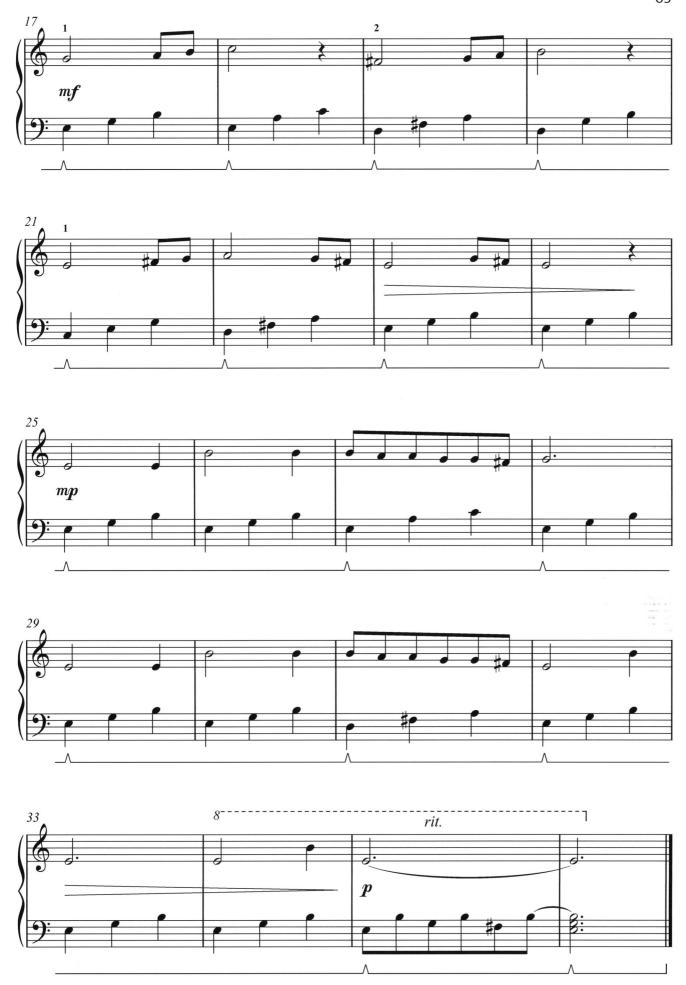